The Board Member's Guide

A BENEFICIAL BESTIARY

by Jeanne H. Bradner

Illustrations by
Carl Granath

CONVERSATION PRESS, INC.
Winnetka, Illinois

TO THE LINCOLN PARK ZOO
in Chicago, where for over 30 years
my family and I have found entertainment,
shared laughter and joy; and,
most important, a renewed perspective
on what it is to be alive and human.

Library of Congress Cataloging-in-Publication Data

Bradner, Jeanne H. (Jeanne Hunt), 1931–
    The board member's guide : a beneficial bestiary / by Jeanne H.
Bradner : illustrations by Carl Granath.
        p.   cm.
    ISBN 0-9634395-3-7. — ISBN 0-9634395-4-5 (pbk.)
    1. Endowments—United States—Officials and employees.
2. Voluntarism—United States.   3. Directors of corporations—United
States.   4. Bestiaries.   I. Title.
HV97.A3873   1995
658.4'22—dc20
                                                    95–41371
                                                        CIP

Contents

Preface

𝒫eople don't go to the zoo often enough! Not only is it fascinating to observe the behavior of the animals, but even more fascinating is the similarity of many of their actions to our own and those of people we know.

𝒴et the significant difference between human beings and animals is that humans have the ability to reflect on their own behavior and change it. In this difference lies our hope and our responsibility.

𝒮o it is in this spirit that this book is written for volunteer board members and the staff who work with them in what, I believe, must — to be successful — be an often frustrating relationship. For from that frustration can come renewal and growth to help board and staff effectively work together with the community to improve the world — or, at least, a small corner of it.

𝓛et us learn from the animals — emulate what is appropriate, change what is not, serve our communities, use our time wisely and accomplish all of this because we have the wisdom and grace to reflect on our behavior and laugh at it. Out of laughter, I believe, can come the courage to improve and persevere!

And So that We Understand Each Other...

Readers of this book will, I hope, come from many areas of interest. They may be involved in social service, arts, religion, education, service clubs, professional groups, government, youth work or countless other important activities. Too often, though, we tend to think of our activity as different, not like "those other groups." We use our special vocabulary, assign our unique titles and separate ourselves from the wisdom that others have learned through time and experience.

The ideas in this book are applicable to all boards of nonprofit organizations and to governmental boards, whether municipal, school, park, library, planning or other. To help clarify special applications, I have used the word "charitable" for boards when I am specifically speaking to those 50l(c)(3) organizations that enjoy a status that allows contributions to be deducted from the donor's income tax. While legal responsibilities may vary, the behaviors I refer to throughout are, I believe, applicable to any group of people who come together on business, nonprofit or government boards and the offshoots thereof, such as advisory groups and committees.

*W*hen I use the words "executive director," I am referring to the chief administrator of the organization. When I use the word "board chair," I am referring to the chief elected officer of the organization.

*T*hroughout the text I have distinguished between "board" and "staff." I realize that in some organizations "staff" may be very small, or even nonexistent. In such cases, board members may, in fact, function as staff much of the time. The challenge of understanding the difference in roles — that boards govern and staff administer — remains just as important. When board members are acting as staff they must remember to implement the policies which have been set by the board and not to take it on themselves individually to create new policies without board concurrence.

The
Board Member's
Guide

1

Joining the Board

Υou are invited to serve on the board of an organization — religious, fraternal, governmental, educational, social service, professional, cultural. You accept because the cause is close to your heart, you want to help the organization to do an even better job and, yes, you are flattered that you are perceived as someone who can help guide the organization through conflicts, decisions and crises. But you go to a few meetings and find yourself confused about your role. Have you talked too much or not enough? Should you react to everything that you disagree with or only to "important" issues? What issues are "important"? Are you in danger of spending a whole term on the board and not finding anything "important" enough to react to? Or, on the other hand, are you going to be the one whom everyone talks about after the meeting — "Well, as usual, we didn't get anything done because 'you know who' talked all the time!"

$\mathcal{H}$uman interaction can be chaotic and frustrating; or it can be productive and exhilarating. Whether your board service is a trip through the jungle, threatened by strange noises and uncomprehended threats; a stroll through the zoo, marked by the sometimes amusing, sometimes irritating behavior of board colleagues; or a rewarding journey to worthwhile social goals may well depend on how clearly you grasp and perform the functions required of an effective board member.

This illustrates why all boards need, and board members should demand, an orientation session. It's important to learn in advance as much about the organization as possible and to understand at the start the job description of a board member.

Nobody was born knowing exactly what the role of a board member is, and many boards go on for years without ever knowing it or trying to find out. Time is well spent defining the job descriptions of board and staff before trying to deal with the trade-offs, complexities and ambiguities of issues and decisions.

Equally important, understanding the role which you and your board colleagues have taken on will help you deal with the variety of human behavior you are about to encounter.

2

What Is a Board Member?

The Lion

The lion is "king of the beasts." Perhaps one reason for his powerful and exalted status is that he understands the difference between policy and implementation. His mission is clear: self preservation. In order to fulfill that mission, he has a stated goal of at least one good meal a day. He delegates implementation of that goal to his executive director — his mate — chosen, in part, for her MDA degree: Management of Delicious Animals. He does not stand over his mate and tell her how to find or prepare the delicious animal, but he stands ready to evaluate her performance. If she fails, she will be subjected to the roaring displeasure that can come from a policy maker with an empty stomach.

*W*hat is a board member? A board member is a trustee, holding in trust the organization — its programs, personnel and property — for its membership, donors, clients, community and the taxpayers. It is important to remember the interest of the taxpayers. Taxpayers are the "donors" for governmental boards; but, in addition, tax-exempt nonprofits sometimes overlook the fact that they are also accountable to taxpayers who compensate via their own taxes for the tax advantage these organizations enjoy.

*B*ecause of these responsibilities, a board member must constantly examine and justify the mission of the organization. Why does the organization exist? What does it do that is important? Is it still relevant to the needs of the community? Should it be doing something else?

Why do we exist?

A favorite exercise of mine is to ask members of a board to write down the mission of the organization. I ask them not to search for it in the bylaws or brochures, but to write down what they believe the mission is — what they would say to someone who asks them in the elevator for a definition of the X-organization. Between the first and the 10th floor, come up with some language that will let the person know what is really special about your organization . . . what makes you feel passionate enough about it to spend time with it, to ask others to support it and to contribute money.

I then have board members read their statements, and we post them around the wall and begin to see the differences in the way members of the board perceive the purpose of the organization. Then we consult the mission statement that is in the bylaws and see if the board really does agree with it. If not, a committee is formed to work on the mission statement and bring it back to the board for more discussion so that everyone can become dedicated to the same purpose.

*T*ry enlarging your board's mission statement on a big poster board and put it on the wall in the board room. Refer to it from time to time at board meetings. It will help keep the discussion on track. It will help decide what is important and what is not.

Whose job is it?

*J*ob descriptions for board members state that board members make policy; staff implement it — but it isn't always easy to decide what is policy and what is implementation. Further, staff does research policy options and make recommendations; and boards, particularly in small organizations with little staff, may be required to help implement policy. Each must be careful: board cannot allow staff to take over policy decisions, and board members who are working side by side with staff need to take off their judgmental board hat and replace it with a team-member staff hat. (Roles are not always as clear-cut as they are for the lions!)

"*V*alues" and "principles" are helpful words to keep in mind when deciding what is policy. What do we value in this organization, in the context of our mission statement? These values can form the basis for policy statements that can help both board and staff make decisions. For example, "We believe this town should protect and maintain its green space"; or "We believe our services should be available to those who cannot afford these services elsewhere in the community."

*O*ne can also view policies as statements of "ends," not of means. The means are usually left to staff to work out and present to the board for approval.

A policy decision is not what color napkins to use at the benefit cocktail party or how to arrange the furniture in the office. But it will be a policy decision to decide whether the funds from the benefit will go to the general fund or to start or amplify a program initiative. And it will be a policy decision to decide if the new office will be downtown or in the community served. It will be a policy decision to examine the budget for that office and make sure it reflects the values the board says it believes in.

3

What Business Are We In?

The Hen

A laying hen sits on her nest — to her the only nest there is. She cackles mightily, celebrating her own achievement, which she seems to believe is unique. Poor parochial fowl, she doesn't know that it takes more than one egg to make a soufflé and more than one person's experience to form collective wisdom.

Gaining experience in one community or on one board can be valuable, but that experience doesn't guarantee that the decisions to be made on another board are going to be any easier. Every board is in a slightly different business. For all, improving the community is a goal; but each board has its own culture and focus. People who believe the experiences they have had on another board, in business or their profession can be transferred in whole often make process difficult. They tend to over-generalize and over-simplify, based solely on their own experiences.

The best board members have a growing edge. They work toward renewal of their organizations, constantly examining and reexamining the business and the mission to adjust them to today's needs. They know the pace of change is so fast that next year, or even next month, they may have to change again. They are not disturbed by this process because they view their organizations as living organisms which must grow and change or die.

We must never despair because "we can't get it right." We should be glad we understand that it isn't completely right; that things are always going out of balance — try as we might; and be glad that we have the perception to see that. We don't want to be caught, like our hen, in a self-satisfied and limited (should we say smug?) frame of mind.

It is for this reason that board members do spend their time deliberating about policies, concentrating on ends, not on means. Good board members constantly question their mission; go to meetings in other towns with other agencies; attend conferences; talk to friends who work on other boards; evaluate the diversity and representation of the board itself . . . question and question again. They know perfection is not in their grasp, but constant improvement is.

Our hen is pleased with her personal accomplishment, and a board member should be pleased with his or her accomplishments. This, however, does not justify the assumption that what you are doing is the only, or even the best, way to pursue your goals. Blind adherence to current practices is not constructive. Progress frequently requires change, and creative board members try to find ways to reframe the way things are being done to make sure that the organization is giving maximum service to the community and justifying the faith of donors and supporters.

4

The
Delicate
Balance

The Gorilla

*The keeper never looks the gorilla in
the eye because to make eye contact is to
acknowledge another's presence and
the need to settle who is dominant.
That's what the gorillas do among
themselves: Don't engage, unless you're
prepared to settle on "Who's in charge?"
Do your executive director, board
chair and board members look each
other in the eye, or is a power battle
going on unacknowledged?*

"*W*hat do we have to have a board for anyway?" That's a question I've heard from staff members, particularly about ten days before a board meeting when they are preparing numerous reports for the board. "They probably won't even read this stuff!" Board members, on the other hand, proclaim that staff members withhold information and only care about protecting their jobs.

*T*here must be a delicate balance between the board chair, board members and the executive director; but none should seek dominance over the other. Rather, they are partners — each fulfilling a necessary role that should be complementary to the other. The expertise of staff is a crucial ingredient; but the organization must also have the leadership, community validation and outreach that the board members supply.

I believe there must always be a creative tension between board and staff, and it is important and liberating for all to understand and acknowledge this. After all, you are in business together to improve something, not merely to be friends.

*B*oard members need to walk a fine line between rubber stamping everything staff suggests and meddling in staff work so intensely that staff can't get its work done. After all, board's role is to govern, not to administer. The board needs to delegate the responsibility for administration and staff to the executive director under the protective umbrella of a clearly articulated statement of vision and values. Board then evaluates the executive director on his or her management abilities.

Exercising power

*B*oard members have power to make or prevent change; so every decision, even those avoided, is an exercise of power. When the power of the board stems from an understanding of the mission, a vision of how that mission might become a reality based on the shared values of the board, and an understanding of what it is to govern rather than administer, then that power, together with the talents of competent staff, can become the power of progress.

*T*he staff and board must have a clear understanding of each other's job descriptions in order to keep the lines of authority and responsibility clear. The following is an overview based on good practice. Individual boards may choose to vary from this slightly, based on their size and mission. The important thing, however, is to make conscious and agreed-upon decisions about expectations. Trouble starts when expectations on either side are not clear from the beginning.

A board should devise its own checklist for evaluating the executive director. This document should be based on the mission and goals of the organization. All board members should have an opportunity to share their evaluations, and the board chair should meet with the executive to review the evaluation and to outline specific steps that can be taken to improve operations. This evaluation can and should be mutual, giving the executive an opportunity to evaluate his or her relationships with the board.

The board also should take time to evaluate itself. Based on its plan, how well did the board do in reaching its goals? Are the relevant committees in place? How effective were the committees in meeting their goals? Did each board member contribute some money to the organization? How was attendance? What other constituencies should be represented on the board?

Expectations of the Board Chair

- Understands and articulates the organization's mission.

- Speaks publicly and to the press on behalf of the organization.

- Advocates on behalf of the organization to the community.

- Takes a major role in fund-raising for the organization.

- Appoints committee chairs (for example: program services, resource development, personnel, finance, and bylaws).

- Keeps in touch with committee chairs to make sure work is continuing on target.

- Talks to the executive director on a regular basis and communicates concerns of committee chairs.

- Develops the meeting agenda, in cooperation with the executive director.

- Conducts the meetings.

- Makes sure that executive director is fulfilling all governmental requirements (payroll taxes, 990 and 990A forms for charitable organizations, for example).

- Leads the yearly evaluation of the executive director.

- Encourages increased volunteer involvement in the organization's affairs.

- Makes sure new board members are oriented to the organization and that there is an annual board retreat.

- Prepares the way for new leadership by encouraging the work of the nominating committee and involving people with leadership potential on committees.

- Leads the planning process and keeps the goals the board has set as benchmarks of progress for both board and staff.

Expectations of the Executive Director

- Helps the board frame and articulate the vision for the organization.

- Hires, supervises, and evaluates staff.

- Provides staff liaison for each committee; keeps in touch with the staff and discusses any concerns directly with the board chair.

- Communicates regularly with the board chair, promptly pointing out emergency issues.

- Makes sure that the board chair and board members receive the necessary information to do their job.

- Makes sure all board members receive materials well in advance of regular meetings, including up-to-date and complete financial reports.

- Makes policy recommendations to the board.

- Implements policy and the strategic plan.

- Responsible with board chair for developing meeting agenda, annual planning sessions, annual retreat, and annual fund-raising efforts.

- Submits a recommended annual budget.

- Encourages meaningful and well-managed volunteer involvement in the organization. Regards volunteers as assets who can perform nonpaid staff work that enhances accomplishments and reduces cost.

- Works on collaborative efforts with other organizations whose goals are complementary.

- Makes sure that an annual independent audit is performed and that all legal requirements for the organization are fulfilled.

- Maintains good files of board and committee meeting minutes.

Expectations of Board Members

- Help articulate the board mission and vision.

- Help determine policy.

- Monitor the implementation of policy, the strategic plan, and the success of programs.

- Keep informed about the organization's financial health.

- Approve and monitor the annual budget.

- Hire, evaluate (yearly) and, if necessary, fire the executive director.

- Be familiar with and adhere to the bylaws of the organization.

- Attend all board meetings, the annual meeting, and the board retreat.

- Participate in an orientation session.

- Serve on at least one committee.

- Read all materials before attending a board meeting.

- Hold in confidence within the board personal information learned about clients, members, staff, or other board members.

- Hold in confidence board discussions of personnel, property negotiations, and legal matters.

- State any conflicts that arise during the member's tenure on the board, and make sure the minutes of the meeting reflect the statement of those conflicts and appropriate abstentions from voting.

- Remember that the member's job is to govern (not administer) in an attitude of reasonable care, honesty, and good faith.

- Understand that the member is legally responsible for the sound management (financial, program, personnel, insurance, and property) of the agency and compliance with governmental regulations.

- Take the initiative and communicate ideas to the board chair.

- Share expertise with the organization.

- Don't meddle in staff work but communicate concerns to the board chair of the organization.

- Advocate for the organization with the community.

- Encourage volunteer involvement in the work of the organization.

- Look for new leadership to recommend to the nominating committee and encourage new people to accept if chosen.

- Support organization-sponsored events with money and attendance.

- Contribute to the financial stability of the organization and encourage others to do so.

- Visit organization-sponsored programs.

5

Checking Egos at the Door

The Wolf

The wolf, we are told by author Farley
Mowat in his book Never Cry Wolf,
stakes out his territory by lifting his leg,
leaving his mark for all to contend
with. It's his territory, and don't you forget
it! The disdain for anyone who ventures
into his territory is clear for all to see.
In boards, such territorialism is
the sign of the EXPERT, and woe betide
anyone who ventures into the territory
of his expertise.

*I*t is important to have members of the board who represent different aspects of the community and who bring with them varied skills and backgrounds. They should, however, consider themselves as members of the board team, rather than as representatives of a single area of influence or expertise.

"*O*h, we must have a lawyer on the board," say almost all nominating committees. My retort is, "We need open and thoughtful people on the board. If the lawyer you are thinking of is an open and thoughtful person, by all means — but if you are thinking this is a good way to get free legal advice, don't do it."

*A*ll experts have areas in which they concentrate. An attorney who specializes in patent law probably won't know as much about local government law as the city manager; but if you bring the lawyer on as an "expert," he will feel he has to act like an expert. It is much better to hire the objective legal help from outside the board; or, if you can't afford to hire it, go to a public interest group that serves the area in which your organization works — arts or disabilities, for example — for the expertise needed.

*M*ost important, board members must concentrate on group process and consensus making first rather than trying to impress everyone with their expertise in law, personnel, accounting, fund raising, volunteer management or whatever their area of professional activity is. Most of all, they must be prepared to make suggestions in a spirit of sharing rather than as ways, like our wolf, of establishing their territorial imperatives.

Sometimes board members who are wolves lurk in the office, second guessing everything staff does. These board members may sincerely believe they are performing "oversight"; but, instead, they keep staff from getting work done.

In some cases "wolves" are not on the board but are members of the staff. They think of themselves as "professionals" (and, therefore, "experts") and don't respect volunteers or collective wisdom. The board needs to ask staff for their input but must not be overpowered or in awe of it. Staff, on the other hand, needs to remember that it is their job to advise, but it is the board that gives the consent.

It's dangerous for boards to give up important policy decisions to the "experts" on the board or among the staff. If they are wrong, all board members will be responsible for the decision. It's best on boards to regard all members as equals and staff as informed resources, and encourage everyone to feel free to question anything.

6

Listening

The Zebra

The zebra wears his stripes for all to see.
They, like his ideas, are firmly fixed.
He is skittish at the possibility of new
ideas, even though they might make him
even more attractive and interesting.
He is content while nothing changes;
but approach him with a new
concept and he, his stripes, and all
who follow him are off to the farthest
corner of his pen. Board members
who are zebras are those who seem to
say, "My mind's made up; don't
confuse me with any facts."

Number of Items: 4

Barcode:0000248579161
Title:Godspell [videorecording]
Due:10/22/2018

Barcode:0000247558554
Title:The deer hunter [videorecording]
Due:10/22/2018

Barcode:0000244184271
Title:The board member's guide : a
beneficial bestiary
Due:11/5/2018

Barcode:0000280679648
Title:The make-ahead cook : 8 smart
strategies for dinner tonight
Due:11/5/2018

Your material(s) are due on
the date(s) listed above.

. . .

10/15/2018   7:18 PM

$\mathcal{P}$eople with fixed ideas are so emotionally wedded to their own view of things that they can't sit back and listen to other people's ideas. They find their security in believing that somehow they must be right all the time.

I remember a story about a friend who listened to a very opinionated person give a presentation. Our friend said, "I'm sorry, but I don't understand your position." The combative person repeated the information, word for word, but in a much louder voice, as if he were talking to someone he thought had a hearing disability. Our friend responded calmly, "Well, I hear you better, but I still don't understand you."

$\mathcal{M}$any problems that arise in groups and organizations arise over a communication problem; but too few people understand that communication is a two-way process: it takes one person to talk and another person to listen. The person who believes he or she knows all the answers does not feel the need even to listen to how others are responding.

Creating a vision

$\mathcal{F}$requently the most helpful device with closed-minded people is the board retreat which not only focuses on orientation and job descriptions but on that most important word, "vision." Encouraging a group of board members to talk about "if money were no problem, what would I like to see this organization (this community, this profession) doing," can involve people in dreaming about what could happen rather than dwelling on what has happened. This can help closed-minded members focus and allow them to see there are other ideas — some of which (surprise!) they never thought of before.

Visioning is also the first essential step in the strategic planning process (a board responsibility) so that what we call a plan is not just based on what we did the year before but on what we ought to be doing.

Getting people to share their visions and dreams is an effective way to develop a team spirit because consensus about some things can emerge very quickly. I remember facilitating such a retreat years ago in a small town in Western Illinois. It quickly came about that this group thought what the youth in the community really needed was a youth center, and before the meeting was over, the group had begun to plan what needs assessments, partnerships and collaborations were required. The youth center was needed; a number of people were inspired and energized because they shared the dream, and the youth center became a reality.

$\mathcal{W}$hat a wonderful moment it is when someone timidly puts forth an idea, and three or four other people in the room say, "Oh, yes, I've wanted to do that for a long time." How much more exciting it is to talk about dreams than how much money was spent last month for copy paper!

$\mathcal{B}$oard members need to spend more time talking about ends than means; or, at least, they need to define their ends carefully before they figure out if the means they are using are really going to get them where they want to go. As was pointed out to Alice in Wonderland, if you don't know where you want to go, then it doesn't really matter which direction you take because you're bound to get somewhere!

$\mathcal{R}$etreats are the time to distance the board from the day-to-day decisions and ask the "why" questions. Why does this organization exist? Why is it important to the community? Why should people support it? It is only after answering these questions that we can focus meaningfully on the "what" questions. What can we do better? What can we do to raise more money or increase attendance? What can we do to provide more services to more people?

$\mathcal{A}$ board retreat encourages a climate of comfort and trust among board and staff that isn't always present at board meetings when people are only together for a few hours. When people join a board, they always feel as if they are expected to know everything right away and there isn't always time to ask questions. Retreats allow people to step back from the day-to-day operations, ask those questions, and vision and dream about the importance of the organization.

*I*t is very important, therefore, not to dilute or damage the purpose of the retreat by introducing regular board business — "Just a few things we have to take care of before we go on with the retreat."

*S*uch retreat questions as, "If we had all the money and staff we needed, what would you like to see this organization do over the next five years?" free people from the reflex answer of "We can't afford it" and free them to think about what creative approaches, changing of priorities or trade-offs there might be. Someone has said, "If we do what we always have done, we will get what we always have gotten." It's important to stop and think if what you are getting is good enough and, if not, what changes might be needed to achieve more meaningful goals.

*A*fter analyzing where the board would like to see the organization in five years (the ends), and what needs to happen, the board can begin to talk about the means to do it: changes in programming, changes in staff composition, in marketing, in involving volunteers, in forging collaborative relationships and in the very structure of the board itself. These "hows" become strategic action steps to reach agreed upon goals and visions.

*F*or example, we really don't know what additional talents or community representation we need on the board unless we know what it is we are trying to do. We don't know what our committee structure should be unless we know what we are trying to achieve.

*E*nds or "whats" should be discussed first; then means or "hows," so that we will know for sure what it is we want to be serious about. Out of this process can come a strategic plan that everyone will believe in and therefore support.

*T*he retreat is not the end of this process. Time needs to be set aside every few months during the board meeting to review the goals and objectives set forth in the organization's plan. The chair of a board I served on taped newsprint around the wall and asked each committee chair to list all the things that had happened in the last months and to star those that were important steps to implementing the strategic plan. This sent everyone scurrying to read the appropriate section of the plan and made it a live and useful document — as it should be.

7

Difficult People

The Bear

The bear looks warm and furry,
maybe even cuddly. He is calm and
unthreatening when left alone.
But, remember, the bear sleeps for
months at a time, then wakes up both
hungry and angry. Don't get in his
way at that time, or you'll have a very
unpleasant experience. He, and
no one else, will set the agenda for
when he works, when he sleeps,
and what he will do when he does it.
It's hard to work cooperatively with
a bear for a board member.

$\mathcal{A}$ bear can be a very difficult board member to handle because, while he appears to be sleeping, he is merely waiting to pounce when his area of personal interest is invaded. Frequently bears come on the board not to give community service but for their own reasons. Perhaps they have had a bad experience with the organization, and they want to "straighten it out." Perhaps they want to use their board position as a stepping stone for personal advantage. Or perhaps they truly believe (as often do those who are elected to public boards) that they, and only they, have a mandate from their public to make a change in a specific area that only they are capable of comprehending.

$\mathcal{S}$o a bear will doze as the board discusses all the "unimportant" (in his view) things but will growl, snarl and try to intimidate anyone who ventures into his personal lair. When it comes to the subject he cares about, he believes he knows all the answers and "collaboration" and "consensus" are not words in his vocabulary.

Dealing with difficult people

$\mathcal{A}$ person who is a bear may be heavily afflicted with a case of personalized power. In his area of interest, the bear believes, there is no room for a "win/win" solution; it must be an "I win/you lose" outcome. Such people can be successful trial lawyers but can be very hard to work with on a board.

To avoid being a bear, board members must remember that most issues that boards deal with are not stark black and white, but are shades of gray. It takes thoughtful discussion, sharing of ideas and information, as well as a values search, to find an answer. Of course, there are occasionally matters of principle so clear that a board member must challenge them, be tenacious in approach and even be accused of being too assertive. But an effective board member chooses very carefully the times when he or she assumes this posture. A board member is much more credible in making this kind of point if he or she is perceived as having been sensitive to other people's opinions in the past.

People who know how to work with others and who are able to prioritize the importance of issues know that sometimes we accommodate others' points of view when issues are important to them and not to us; sometimes we avoid issues that are not important or not timely; sometimes we compromise with others on issues where there are equally valid points of view; and, most important, at all times, we are perceived as being willing to cooperate.

Cooperation comes from taking time to listen to others; changing our opinions based on better information; and a willingness to live with principled consensus because we know that a group can and will accomplish something they have all had a voice in creating.

Bears who sleep through the minute-by-minute work of the board and only growl loudly when certain issues are broached are not constructive or appealing board members.

8

Nitpicking

The Monkey

*The monkey sits with a serious look on
her face, but what she really is
concentrating on is picking fleas off
her neighbor. Disturb that concentration
on the trivial, and she suddenly is
off to another portion of the cage where
she can sit undistracted. She chatters
at random and without regard to what
anyone else is saying. From time
to time she suddenly leaps into wild
swings from position to position,
often returning to the place from
which she started.*

$\mathcal{T}$riviality is the curse of the board member who is confused about his or her job description and who doesn't grasp the big picture (the mission). Board members who want to be conscientious and who haven't benefited from good board orientations and retreats focus on small things to assuage their own conscience. Hence, you have arguments over how many paper clips were purchased last month (a \$25 item), while important policy issues are ignored.

$\mathcal{B}$oard members, it is true, must be reassured that the organization is running well. Normally, this reassurance comes from written reports provided before the board meeting, or the sense of progress provided by committee chairs, the executive director and the board chair. It is not necessary to challenge each item in the treasurer's report just to indicate that the member read it.

$\mathcal{D}$etails that may be of interest can be pursued in a private conversation without taking up the entire board's time. Subtle concerns about performance can and should be discussed with the board chair. Understanding what is routine trivia and what is of legitimate board concern is essential to being an effective member of the board.

$\mathcal{A}$nother evidence of not understanding the big picture is our monkey's unfortunate habit of raising issues, legitimate or not, at the wrong time. A well-constructed agenda has an internal logic of issues and topics. Jumping wildly from topic to topic is destructive of efficient discussion and careful decision making.

$\mathcal{B}$oard members who worry about means more than ends, who don't listen and, most important, who don't feel passionate about the mission of the organization are apt to be the ones who trivialize the business of the board, wasting their own time and the time of the entire board.

9

Meaningful Meetings

The Aviary

The aviary is full of beautiful, chattering birds. Each one sings his own song, seemingly oblivious of his neighbors. Do they ever listen to each other? Does your board meeting ever resemble an aviary?

One reason busy people will say "no" to an invitation to join a board is that they remember all those "meaningless meetings" they have attended in previous board service. Since "busy people" are so often the ones who have a track record of hard work and are, therefore, asked to join boards, they have just cause to be concerned. Indeed, there should be a reason for every committee and board meeting that is held.

This is a key responsibility of board leadership. Routinely copying old agenda formats, encouraging committee chairs to meet before they have needed information and other "automatic pilot" behavior will gradually undermine board attendance and performance.

The Role of the Board Chair

*T*he chair must take concrete steps to make sure meetings are not meaningless.

- Before sending out the meeting notice, the board chair and executive director should carefully discuss what the agenda for the meeting should be. Consult the minutes of the preceding meeting for unresolved issues and discussions. Make sure those are addressed. Evaluate what has happened between meetings and decide which new issues the board must consider.

- Concise materials for meetings should be mailed out in time for them to be reviewed by board members; and members should be encouraged to do so. Sometimes just pointing out that the question asked at a board meeting was answered in the previously mailed materials is a way to encourage board members to do the homework for the next meeting.

- Expect committees to meet between board meetings to proceed with their assignments such as program services, marketing, personnel, finance or fund-raising. A committee acts as a clearinghouse for emerging and continuing issues that fall under its job description and discusses ways to approach problems and achieve outcomes. It then brings policy recommendations to the board for decision.

- Avoid the dreary habit of having each and every committee chair report, whether or not he or she has anything to say. Confine committee reports to those items on which group decisions need to be made. Don't take time at the board meeting for a blow-by-blow summary of each committee meeting. Put committee reports in writing and ask board members to read them during out-of-meeting time.

- A well-prepared board chair knows before the meeting begins what issues are to be discussed and what recommendations or decisions need to be made. The chair does not know exactly what those decisions or recommendations might be, though the chair may have a recommendation to offer. But he or she believes that these are open-ended issues which merit discussion and resolution. Good chairs are not dictators; but they are facilitators — facilitators with goals who develop techniques to move the meeting along and, at the same time, allow discussion.

- A good chair needs to arrange the agenda so that the most time can be spent on the most significant issues. Frequently that means putting those issues first on the agenda before board members get tired. In order not to prejudice the discussion and to allow a good exchange of ideas, good chairs refrain from stating their own opinions first.

- Good chairs encourage everyone to talk in turn and ask others to listen. Perhaps there is no time when a gavel is more useful than to say, "One person at a time, please." Or "There is only one meeting going on here" (a useful device when board members start small side discussions).

- Good chairs know that when issues seem irresolvable or more information is needed, that issue needs to be referred back to the committee and brought to the next meeting.

- Good chairs are not intimidated by Robert's Rules of Order. For the average board meeting, Robert's Rules are merely a time-tested system to facilitate meetings by considering one thing at a time. In an informal setting, there is some discussion and generation of alternative ideas. Then there is a motion and a second on an alternative that has begun to take an appealing shape; the motion is discussed and voted on, unless there is an amendment. If there is an amendment, the amendment is discussed and voted on before the motion. If there is an amendment to an amendment, it is discussed and voted on before the amendment and the motion. This simplifies discussion and makes it easier for everyone.

Robert's Rules become more sophisticated in their use by legislative bodies which frequently use parliamentary maneuvers to achieve partisan ends. This is fascinating to students of parliamentary procedure but usually is not part of the process on a voluntary board of directors.

Skills That Help Groups

$\mathcal{E}$ach board member has the responsibility
to make the meeting meaningful for all.
Good board members believe in collaboration,
democratic process and collective wisdom.
They also develop their skills to work with
others.

- Encouraging — "That was a good idea."

- Expressing one's own feelings about an idea
  — not "That is dumb," but "That approach
  makes me uneasy."

- Mission reminding — "Does this fulfill our
  mission, our goals?" (Otherwise known as
  "keeping an eye on the ball.")

- Consensus testing — "It seems to me we all
  agree about . . . "

- Information — Giving facts and figures that
  are needed.

- Listening — Too often board members are
  thinking about what they are going to say
  rather than listening to what is being said.

- Expanding — Don't repeat what has already
  been said. If there is something that needs to
  be added, add it.

- Summarizing — This is important for the
  chair to do, but individual board members

can be helpful in trying to pull a wide-ranging discussion together.

- Contributing — Board members should contribute their ideas; better to say it than to wish later that you had.

Styles That Impede Groups

Good board members avoid the following:

- Personal Attacks — Attack the problem, not the person.

- Stubbornness — "I don't think you heard what I said; so I'll say it again, but louder."

- "Uncle Harry" Stories — Interpreting an entire issue in the light of what happened to one person at one time.

- Frivolity — A good joke or "bon mot" at the right time is wonderful and can frequently ease the tension when emotions are high or simply add to the pleasant dynamic of the board; but someone who jokes all the time isn't taking the meeting or his or her responsibilities seriously.

- Dominating — Even though you may be an expert on an issue, let someone else have a chance to develop ideas.

- False self-deprecation — "Well, I may not know all the answers; but . . . " Who in the room has all the answers? And does this imply that anyone who disagrees is asserting that he or she does have all the answers? Under this goes, the "Well, I'm just a housewife," or "I'm not a professional," and so on.

- Self-righteousness — "Well, I'm just trying to be fair" . . . implying that he or she is the only fair-minded person in the room.

- Parochialism — "What is good for my neighborhood or my discipline is good for everyone." Maybe "yes," maybe "no." What has been done may, indeed, be good for a particular place or group, but it needs to be put in context for the unit we are now addressing.

10

Being
There Is
Not
Enough

The Giraffe

The giraffe searches for leaves
(like ideas) high among the trees.
He doesn't listen to others nor does he
speak. He's there, but he's in his
own world. Perhaps he is shy; perhaps
he feels his ideas are too fine for
his fellow zoo mates; or perhaps he
fears he may demonstrate the
oft-quoted statement, "I would rather
keep my mouth closed and have
people think me stupid, than open it
and remove all doubt."

$\mathcal{A}$t a minimum, board members should try to attend all meetings of the board and the committees to which they belong. Why?

$\mathcal{W}$hen a person says "yes" to board membership, he or she is embracing a responsibility. The very least a board member can do is to set aside time on the calendar (make sure there is an advance calendar of board meeting dates) to attend the meetings of the board. Obviously, there are times when paying jobs, sickness or family responsibilities will have to take precedence. But those should be kept to a minimum. My own rule of thumb is that if a person misses three consecutive board meetings, that person should resign from the board.

$\mathcal{W}$hen board members have miraculous and occasional appearances at board meetings, they need to be filled in on what happened before. Sometimes they will disagree with actions taken previously and disrupt the whole consensus process. That is not fair to those who have been in regular attendance and have worked through the problems (perhaps, by their light, ad nauseam).

$\mathcal{S}$o, our giraffe is at least off to a good start because he is there . . . but that is not enough.

Board members have an obligation to participate, to join in the debate, to raise new ideas and to share personal experiences. The meeting chair should encourage participation, turning to the quiet person and saying, "What do you think?"

What makes a board a remarkable vehicle for guiding an organization is the collective wisdom of its members and the group authority they represent on behalf of the community. Yes, it's often frustrating to advance a contrary opinion and be put down (or worse) ignored by the group. But board members must keep trying and participating; for the very idea that a board member may be loath to offer ("Maybe they'll think I'm stupid") can be the idea that will change the course of the organization. Sometimes a board member will recognize this by the significant pause that happens while everyone sorts out the idea and thinks, "Why didn't I say that?"

Remember, board members are together to examine principles, not trivia; to attack problems, not each other; and to evolve a mutual and effective vision of progress.

Don't be patronizing

Sometimes quiet people aren't shy . . . they are bored. They feel they know it all, or have been there before — in short, they are patronizing. Good members share their knowledge and their expertise, without taking over the debate. An attitude of "Poor little dears; I'll be quiet, and they will come to their senses" doesn't help group process. Sometimes such people really just want to reserve judgment and don't participate so that later they can pretend they had nothing to do with the decision. When one is part of group process, silence is considered assent!

11

Time Management

The Hippo

The hippo loves his bath, rollicking in glorious mud. He splashes and plays, certainly not getting any cleaner, but the energy he expends is impressive. He's really having fun, but there's no room for anyone else in the mud while he's there. Like some board members, he clearly cares more about "foam" than substance.

$\mathcal{B}$oard members who haven't figured out their purpose and bought into the mission of the organization can be like our hippo. Oh, they may be very busy, but is their busyness getting them anywhere? Board members need to think about making the most of their time on the board: "Am I using my time constructively? Am I spending it on the most important items? What is really important for me and my talents to accomplish on behalf of this board?" Doing first things first and starting with the end (the mission) in mind are ways to make a contribution that has "substance."

Outcome-based evaluation

$\mathcal{T}$hose who truly believe that substance is more important than form are demanding outcome-based evaluations of their programs. They know it's not enough to have a program and to learn that 500 telephone calls were received and responded to. This is a good "process" (form) evaluation, but organizations need to know the outcomes from those calls. How many people actually benefited from the organization's services in response to these calls and how?

$\mathcal{A}$ board member from a literacy agency might ask "What did we do this past quarter to improve people's ability to read; and how can we prove we did it?" Board members need to work with each other and staff to analyze what they believe would be successful outcomes from their work and find ways to measure those outcomes over a reasonable period of time. Pre- and post-tests, focus groups, interviews, community or audience surveys are all possibilities; but the appropriate method has to be chosen to meet the definition of "success" for the program. Not only is there satisfaction in this for the board and staff, but it is powerful ammunition with potential donors and reassures board, direct-service volunteers and staff that the work they have contributed to has meaning. Even more important, though, it is a way to monitor progress and to make corrections in programming when the outcomes are not good enough.

Board can spend a lot of time quarreling about minor expenses, without analyzing what outcomes the major portion of budgeted money bought. That is one of the most significant "ends" questions there is.

12

Terms of Office

The Elephant

The elephant looks tired and wrinkled.
She moves slowly and spends hours
sweeping dry old hay into her mouth,
showing no emotion and no enthusiasm.
Is that because she never forgets
anything and she can never escape the
past? Poor elephant, she is doomed
to remember what others have forgotten.
Fortunately, though, unlike her
human counterpart, she can't say,
"We tried that once, but it didn't work."

*I*nstitutional memory is valuable for an organization. Some of it exists in minutes, policy handbooks and by-laws, and these can and must be consulted. Much "institutional memory," however, exists in the recollections and experience of board members. Properly offered, as one but not the definitive consideration, such memory can be helpful to a board's understanding of current issues.

*P*ossession of "institutional memory" by itself, however, is not a qualification for board membership. In fact, sometimes board members who stay on the board endlessly because of their "institutional memory" can be a negative influence.

*T*o guard not just against this possibility but also against stagnation of many kinds, it is important to have staggered terms for board members — two to four years, for example, renewable for one or two terms — so that the organization benefits from both continuity and the opportunity for new people to join the board.

*W*hile on a rare occasion, it may be necessary for the immediate past president to stay on the board, usually it is best for him or her to leave because of the temptation to say (as our elephant cannot), "We tried that once and it didn't work." An idea that might not have been successful at one time in history can be extraordinarily successful at another time.

*P*ast presidents and board members can continue to serve on committees or honorary or advisory boards. They can also have a sabbatical term from the board and then return to it. But boards need a fresh sprinkling of new membership, community representation and ideas. No one should have (or should want) a lifetime seat on a board.

*T*he number of board members should be analyzed, too. Often organizations put lots of people on in the hope of raising money from them. Or, in all-volunteer or small staff organizations, every worker is given a spot on the board. However, a board of more than 25 people will have difficulty becoming a productive governance body. It can become a pawn (because of size and the difficulty of communication and genuine involvement) of the paid staff. Sizes of boards vary, of course, by organization, precedent and law. Local government groups usually have few members; but large budget nonprofits sometimes have as many as 40 people on the board. Forty is unmanageable and encourages absenteeism.

13

Remember to Ask "Why?"

The Owl

The owl keeps saying "who? who?"
and people think him wise. You
can't see him clearly, but his mysterious
presence is felt by those around him.
The owl never says "why? why?"
perhaps because he is most concerned
about who will do a task — certainly
not him — than if it implements
policy. He just hides in the shadows
of the night and lets others take the
chance of stepping into the light.

Perhaps the most important question a board member can ask is "why?" Why do we want to do this? Why do we want to spend this money? Why are we ignoring our goals, our mission, our policies?

Moving to the "how" questions or the "who will do it?" questions before answering the "why" questions can be very dangerous. It is like deciding where we will fight the first battle before we have made the very important decision as to whether we really want to declare war.

The wise board member who is convinced of the "why" can be the most useful member in terms of advocacy. That member can make presentations to the legislature, funders and the community about why the organization is effective. "Why" people usually have the passion to inspire others.

In addition, "why" people are generous givers and inspire others to give because they understand the significance of the organization and its reason for being. Not only are "why" people good at raising money, they are good at raising in-kind resources, including recruiting other volunteers to help the organization.

*I*ndeed, people dedicated to the "why" probably won't ask "who?" They will, because of their commitment, become personally involved.

14

Don't Get Snakebite

The Snake

*The snake slithers on his belly,
moving quietly to destinations only he
understands. The wavy motion of his
body and the cold look in his eye
make it difficult to tell where he is going.
He does not speak but introduces himself
with a bite which may be poisonous.
The first snake was doomed to crawl on
his belly for eternity so all could
identify him, but the snakes in your
organization may not be so easy
to recognize!*

$\mathcal{W}$e all work hard to have productive relationships with other people, to try to understand their values and their needs, and involve them in decision making. But sometimes there are those people who frustrate all of our efforts to invite them into a collaborative relationship. Usually these people eventually turn everyone off, but that takes time because each new member of the group believes that somehow he or she can figure out how to work with old George or Georgina; in the process, lots of time and energy are wasted.

$\mathcal{W}$hat are some of the snakes we find on boards? They are board members who:

- Are unwilling to compromise over anything, any time.

- Won't abide by the consensus of the group, taking their positions to the public or the press.

- Reveal confidential information.

- Exert personalized power by being completely unpredictable, voting against a concept one time and for it another, with equal passion and personal rectitude.

- Agree with the board chair and the committee chair in advance that they support a particular position and then not only vote against it but launch a personalized attack against the idea and the people proposing it.

- Spring strategic "surprises" at board meetings. These are items that could have been brought to the attention of the board chair in advance; but snakes purposely "spring" them as a tactic to overwhelm, disarm or divide (and conquer, if they can).

- Take personally a loss on a policy question they recommended and therefore vote against the next issue not because of the issue but because it is proposed by someone who voted against them previously.

- Do not declare a conflict of interest. (This is reason for unseating a board member.)

- Receive material profit (other than reimbursement for reasonable expenses) from membership on the board.

- Ask a staff member to give an opinion about another staff member.

- Ask a staff member to drop the regular workload to do a big job, without clearing it with the executive director or the committee chair with whom that staff member works.

- Become a personal court of appeal for individual staff members, rather than referring staff problems to the board chair or executive director.

15

Boards and the Law

The Eagle

*Sharp-eyed and high-flown, the eagle
watches what goes on from above.
When he spots an error in the making,
he swoops down to seize the mistake
and raise it high for all to see.
All board members and staff must
become legal eagles on behalf of their
organizations.*

*I*n local government boards, the legal issues are the laws and ordinances of the local unit, as well as the state and federal laws that apply.

*N*onprofits are accountable to the laws of the state in which they are incorporated and to the appropriate regulations of the federal government. 501(c) organizations have special regulations and rules and need to be alertly aware of what is required of their specific Internal Revenue Service category. 50l(c)(3) organizations have a special privilege so that donors can claim tax deductions for gifts. Therefore, 50l(c)(3)s must have boards who follow the regulations scrupulously; otherwise, they risk losing this special status.

*M*any states today have enacted laws limiting the liability of nonprofit boards to acts that are willful and wanton. Boards need to research these laws in their states and determine what protection they offer. In addition, boards must provide necessary insurance coverage and good risk management for the board, the volunteers, the staff and the organization as a whole.

*S*ome of the items that nonprofit boards need to be aware of are requirements their organization must meet for:

- Withholding and reporting payroll taxes on the required federal and state forms.

- Filing 990 forms; and, for 501(c)3 organizations, 990A forms, with the Internal Revenue Service.

- Meeting requirements for reporting Unrelated Business Income.

- Reporting on employee benefit plans.

- Filing any annual reports required by the state.

- Complying with state laws covering unemployment and workers' compensation insurance.

- Complying with any state or local laws on solicitation of funds, land use or zoning.

- Respecting requirements that limit lobbying and political activity.

- Adhering to all government requirements pertaining to any government grants a charitable organization has obtained. For federal grants, there are Office of Management and Budget rules which apply and should be followed.

- Arranging for a yearly independent audit.

- Practicing good financial management. For example, the person signing the check should not be the person reconciling the bank statement.

- Assuring that staff compensation and professional consulting fees are reasonable; and providing for sound investment of any funds not expended.

$\mathcal{T}$he national organization, Accountants for the Public Interest, can be very helpful to groups which have any questions about this, as can the state office with which your Articles of Incorporation are filed, your State Department of Labor, Secretary of State, Attorney General and the United States Internal Revenue Office.

16

Collaboration

The Harbor Seal

*The seal is always in motion yet never
seems to be working very hard.
There is nothing spectacular about his
coloring nor any show of strength
or ferocity. Easy but powerful flipper
strokes propel him rapidly through
the water, up and down, around and
around. The seal is intent on
"doing his thing," yet he never collides
with the other seals who are
"doing their things." He has a sense of
where he's going and where they're
going and how they can all get
there without a collision. Seals can
make great board members.*

The joy of successful board membership is sharing a mission and experiencing the wisdom that can come from thoughtful and honest group decision making. Listening, respecting, contributing are all part of the process. Keeping an eye on the mission, following the strategic plan and commitment to the role the organization has in making the community a better place in which to live keep good board members from triviality and over-personalizing decisions and debates.

Creating a path for others

Like our seal, good board members create a path for others — particularly for new leadership. They make their contribution, fill their role, but welcome and encourage the participation of the bright stars on the horizon who may come in with new energy and new ideas to move the organization ahead. Board members who are seals know that the new people may not move exactly in the same direction they do; but they know that the environment is always changing and that sometimes new directions keep us off a collision course with change.

If someone says to current leadership, "We can't get along without you," current leadership should not be so much complimented as troubled, because part of the job of leadership is to encourage new leaders. This is the process of renewal and growth; and, if board members have the future of the organization at heart, it is an essential thing to do.

17

The Peaceable Kingdom

"Then the wolf shall live with the sheep and the leopard lie down with the kid; the calf and the young lion shall grow up together." Isaiah 11:6

Though we probably won't see the ideal of the prophet in this world, good faith and a joint mission can enable our animals' human counterparts to understand each other and to lay aside their self-serving and egotistical instincts. It is not really that difficult for the monkey to grasp the lion's understanding of mission. The gorillas can exist in communal harmony, the hen can broaden her vision of the world and the zebra can learn to entertain a new idea.

Unlike the jungle, where each species is on its own, our board "zoo" can learn to work together for significant ends. By understanding themselves and each other, board members can join in a synergistic enterprise where the whole can be greater than we dared to dream because of its many-faceted, individual parts.

This is what is meant by the word "civilization."

ORDER INFORMATION

Copies of *The Board Member's Guide* can be ordered directly from Conversation Press, Inc.

You may call 1-800-848-5224 with your Visa or MasterCard ready.

Or you may send your check (made payable to "Conversation Press, Inc.") and order to Box 172, Winnetka, IL 60093.

A single copy of the paperback edition is $9.95 plus $2.00 for shipping and handling. Illinois residents should add $.77 for sales tax.

The hardcover edition is $14.95, plus $2.00 for shipping and handling. The Illinois sales tax is $1.16.

Call 1-800-848-5224 to inquire about quantity discounts and shipping charges for multiple-copy orders.